# GraphQL API Design

Matthias Biehl

Second edition:    April 2018

Biehl, Matthias
    API-University Press
    Volume 5 of the API-University Series.
    Includes illustrations, bibliographical references and index.
    ISBN-13: 978-1979717526
    ISBN-10: 1979717524

API-University Press
http://www.api-university.com
info@api-university.com

# Contents

.

# Abstract

Want to build APIs like Facebook? Since Facebook's framework for building APIs, GraphQL, has become publicly available, this ambition seems to be within reach for many companies. And that is great. But first, let's learn what GraphQL really is and – maybe even more importantly – let's figure out how to apply GraphQL to build APIs that consumers love.

In this book, we take a hands-on approach to learning GraphQL. We first explore the concepts of the two GraphQL languages using examples. Then we start writing some code for our first GraphQL API. We develop this API step by step, from creating a schema and resolving queries, over mocking data and connecting data sources all the way to developing mutations and setting up event subscriptions.

Are your API consumers important to you? This book shows you how to apply a consumer-oriented design process for GraphQL APIs, so you can deliver what your consumers really want: an API that solves their problems and offers a great developer experience.

Do you want to enable the API consumers so they can build great apps? This book explains the GraphQL query language, which allows the API consumers to retrieve data, write data and get notified when data changes. More importantly, you let them decide, which data they really need from the API.

Do you want to make your API easy and intuitive to use? This book shows you how to use the GraphQL schema language to define a type system for your API, which serves as a reference documentation and helps your API consumers write queries that are syntactically correct.

Do you want to profit from what has worked for others? This book provides a collection of best practices for GraphQL that have worked for other companies, e.g. regarding pagination, authentication and caching.

GraphQL and REST are competing philosophies for building APIs. It is not in the scope of this book to compare or discuss the two approaches. The focus of this book is on a hands-on approach for learning GraphQL.

# 1 GraphQL Introduction

## 1.1 What is an API?

Modern applications are typically *distributed systems*, consisting of a *frontend* and a *backend*. The frontend displays the user interface, with its icons, buttons, and graphics. It may be a web site, a mobile app, or a voice-based app. The backend stores and delivers the business data. It is typically realized on an application server.

Frontend and backend run on different machines, but the data, which is managed by the backend systems, needs to be delivered to the frontend systems, where it is displayed. To manage the communication between frontend and backend, an API, short for *application programming interface*, is introduced. In this pattern, the backend serves the API, the frontend consumes the API. To realize this pattern, an API server needs to be built on the backend-side and an API client is built on the frontend-side.

But first, let's have a look at the interaction between frontend and backend. In which ways may the frontend interact with the backend? The frontend may

- retrieve data from the backend

- write new data to the backend or update data on the backend

- get notified by the backend, as soon as the data on the backend changes

These needs of frontends regarding the interaction with backends are quite universal. Thus, a couple of philosophies, such as RPC, SOAP, REST, and GraphQL, have been developed to structure the interaction between frontend and backend.

## 1.2 What is GraphQL?

GraphQL allows us to build APIs for retrieving data, writing data and getting notified when data changes. GraphQL provides a new philosophy for building APIs, which helps us to structure the interaction between frontend and backend. To structure the interaction, GraphQL offers three things: a declarative, typed query language for APIs (see section 1.2.1), a schema language for specifying data structures (see section 1.2.2) and a runtime for building APIs (see section 1.2.3).

GraphQL was originally developed as proprietary technology by Facebook, but was open-sourced in 2015 and is now licensed under the Open Web Foundation Agreement (OWFa). The GraphQL specification is available in the form of a working draft [6].

### 1.2.1 GraphQL Query Language

GraphQL offers a *query language* for APIs. The language allows the frontend to interact with the backend. The language provides primitives for retrieving data, writing data and getting notified when data changes.

The GraphQL query language is *declarative*. Another well-known declarative query language is SQL, which is used for interacting with relational database servers. In a declarative language, we specify WHAT we want as a result, and not HOW the result should be computed. We let the server figure out HOW the result is computed. A declarative language provides an appropriate level of abstraction for clients. Clients can interact with the data, without having to worry about backend implementation details. The interaction is easy from the perspective of a client. The heavy lifting needs to be done on the server side.

## 1.2.2 GraphQL Schema Language

GraphQL allows us to define and describe our data structures. For this purpose, GraphQL provides a *typed schema language*. We specify custom types for the data served by the API. A GraphQL schema is created by defining types, which have a number of fields, and by providing access functions for each field and each type.

## 1.2.3 GraphQL Runtime

When implementing the API for our data schema, we use the generic GraphQL runtime. The GraphQL runtime provides an implementation of the common functionality that needs to be provided by all GraphQL APIs. Which features are those? GraphQL APIs have a single endpoint, which can receive and resolve GraphQL queries written in the GraphQL query language (see section 1.2.1). The data served on this endpoint conforms to the schema, which is written in the GraphQL schema language (see section 1.2.2).

By providing an implementation of the common functionality, the GraphQL runtime helps us to build APIs quickly. Nevertheless, the GraphQL runtime does not limit us too much in our implementation. GraphQL can be connected to any backend, such as a host system, a middleware, a SOAP web service, REST API, relational database or NoSQL database[1]. GraphQL

---

[1] There is no link between graph databases (such as Neo4j) and GraphQL.

13

is not tied to any specific database or storage engine.

## 1.3 Why are there Two Languages in GraphQL?

There is a query language and a schema definition language in GraphQL. These two languages have different purposes. The purpose of the schema definition language is to define the structure of the business data exposed by the GraphQL API. API providers use the schema definition language to specify the interface. The purpose of the query language is to interact with the GraphQL endpoint. Clients use the query language for reading data, writing data or subscribing to notifications. The schema serves as a constraint on the possible interactions.

The *GraphQL schema* can be compared to an à-la-carte menu in a restaurant, showing all the delicious dishes that clients may choose from. The menu has been defined by the owner of the restaurant, and it serves as an interface to the backend of the restaurant (a.k.a. kitchen). Ordering dishes that are not on the menu is not possible, simply because the kitchen is not prepared for it.

In this analogy, a *GraphQL query* is comparable to the order a client places in the restaurant. In this order, the client may select certain dishes from the menu, such as a starter and main dish. The same is true in GraphQL: in a GraphQL query, we refer to the elements that have been defined in the GraphQL schema.

## 1.4 What is the Graph in GraphQL?

A graph is a very generic data structure, so it should be possible to express the data of any application in the form of a graph.

And this graph, formed by all application data, is what we call the graph in GraphQL.

With GraphQL we look at the overall set of data that is exposed by an API provider. All this data is exposed via a single endpoint. Compared to REST endpoints, the single GraphQL endpoint exposes a lot of data. This comprehensive set of data with its entities and relationships between the various entities forms the graph of GraphQL. To retrieve any data at all, one needs to navigate the graph.

When using other philosophies for building APIs, such as REST, we usually create several API endpoints and whatever is exposed by any single one of the API endpoints is typically not a generic graph, but rather a single entity or a list of entities. But there can be graph-like relationships across all API endpoints of an API provider. And this is in fact attempted by REST: resources are linked by URLs.

Both philosophies are capable of expressing application data in form of a graph, with GraphQL the graph is more explicit, since it is served on a single endpoint.

## 1.5 A GraphQL Application

A GraphQL application consists of a GraphQL API (see chapter 4), which is part of the backend, and a GraphQL client, which is part of the frontend. The GraphQL client sends GraphQL queries (see chapter 3) to the GraphQL API. The GraphQL API processes queries in the following way:

1. The API receives the request and extracts the query. The query may be bound to HTTP and encoded in a JSON data structure (see chapter 6.1).

2. The API checks and validates the query (see chapter 4.1.1) to ensure it only refers to the types and fields that are

defined in the schema.

3. The API resolves the query to produce a result (see chapter 4.1.2). For this purpose, it may interact with backend systems and databases. The result is typically encoded in JSON and is sent back to the client.

## 1.6 What about REST?

Distributed systems, in general, are built with architectural styles of RPC, SOAP or REST, but when it comes to APIs, REST is the main paradigm. For a long time, REST was even thought to be the only accepted architectural style for building APIs.

Graph QL is neither the same as REST nor is Graph QL an extension of REST nor is Graph QL an improved version of REST. GraphQL provides a new philosophy for realizing APIs. That does not mean that Graph QL replaces REST and pushes it off the stage. There are good reasons to choose a RESTful API design.

GraphQL and REST are competing philosophies for building APIs. Each philosophy has its strong and its weak points. Looking at REST and Graph QL, there are a number of commonalities and major differences. When building a new API, it is a case-by-case decision to go with REST or Graph QL. If you are interested in a discussion on the differences, commonalities, strengths, and weaknesses of REST and Graph QL, check out the book *"REST & Graph QL"* [5].

# 2 GraphQL Schema Language

The GraphQL schema language is central to GraphQL, as it allows us to describe the structure or shape of the graph. The shape of the graph is expressed in the form of a schema. The schema defines a number of types and a number of relations between these types.

## 2.1 GraphQL Schema

Let's study an example of a schema. The schema describes three types (Book, Author, and Query).

```
type Book {
  id: ID!
  title: String
  authors: [Author]
}
type Author {
      id: ID!
      name: String
}
type Query {
  books: [Book]
  book_by_id(id: ID!): Book
}
```

These types are related, i.e. there is s reference from Query to Book and from Book to Author. Another way of putting it, is that they share an edge in the type graph. This type graph is visualized in figure 2.1.

## 2.2 GraphQL Type System

GraphQL queries are strongly typed, based on a type system which is defined by the GraphQL schema (see section 2.1). The

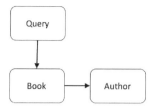

Figure 2.1: Example Type Graph

type system helps in various situations:

- During execution/resolution of a query, the type system helps to determine what to do next.

- When crafting queries, the introspection mechanism provided through the type system, allows us to do syntax-directed editing and guide us with respect to what is possible and available.

This type system consists of *predefined types* and *individual types*. Predefined types are built in to GraphQL, such as the scalar types int, float, boolean and String (see section 2.5). Individual types are defined by a GraphQL schema, using the GraphQL schema language, which we introduce in this chapter.

## 2.3 Types and Fields

A type is identified by its type name (Book or Author in our example in section 2.1) and consists of a number of fields. Our Book type consists of the fields id, title, and authors. Each of these fields has a type: The field id is of type ID, the field title is of type String and the field authors is of type array of Author.

### 2.3.1 Obligatory Fields - Nillable Fields

A field can be marked with an exclamation mark ! to indicate that the field is obligatory, e.g. the field id of type ID within the type Book.

```
type Book {
  id: ID!
  title: String
  authors: [Author]
}
```

If an obligatory field exists within a type, the type cannot be instantiated without providing a value for the obligatory field. In our example, the field id is obligatory for an instance of the type Book; thus the field id will not be null.

Fields that are not obligatory are called *nillable*. Fields in GraphQL are by default nillable, i.e. when fields are not marked with an exclamation mark. In the example above, the fields title and authors are nillable.

## 2.4 Root Types

With GraphQL queries we navigate in a graph. Where do we start navigating in a graph? In a graph, such as the one shown in Figure 2.1, the starting point determines where we can navigate and which nodes we can reach. Depending on where we start and depending on the structure of the graph, we may not be able to navigate all parts of the tree. This may be intentional or not.

In GraphQL we can define the starting points for navigating the tree, by defining fields in the so-called *root types*. A root type is a container for a certain type of operation. GraphQL offers three root types: Query, Mutation, and Subscription. Syntactically, they are just regular types with fields (see section 2.3). What is special about root types, is that they can be used as a starting point when formulating requests in the GraphQL query language (see chapter 3). Each GraphQL implementation must at least define a `Query` type and may define a `Mutation` and `Subscription` type.

```
type Query {
  books: [Book]
  book(title:String!): Book
  book_by_id(id:ID!): Book
}

type Mutation {
  addBook(title: String!): Book
}

type Subscription {
  bookAdded: Book
}
```

## 2.5 Scalar Types

Many *scalar types* are built-in to GraphQL, just as for any programming language. They comprise `int`, `float`, `boolean` and `String`. In addition, there is the built-in scalar type `ID`, which is used to uniquely identify an object.

```
scalar Isbn
type Book {
  id: ID!
  isbn: Isbn
  title: String
  authors: [Author]
}
```

Besides the built-in scalar types , it is possible to define and use custom scalar types , such as `Isbn` in the example above. Custom scalar types need to provide a serialization function and a parsing function. The execution semantics for such scalar types needs to be implemented in the resolver functions (see section 4.1.2).

## 2.6 Array

An *array* is used to express a list of objects of the same type. Arrays can be applied to scalar types and for object types, e.g

[int] for a list of integers or [Book] for a list of **Books**. Arrays are used in GraphQL just as in any programming language.

## 2.7 Enum

An *enum* type has a limited set of values it can possibly take on. Defining the enum actually means defining this finite list of possible values. In the following example, the enum **TrafficLight** can take on any of the value RED, GREEN or YELLOW.

```
enum trafficLight{
  RED
  GREEN
  YELLOW
}
```

## 2.8 Interface

An *interface* is similar to a type definition, it defines a list of fields, but it is different, since it cannot be instantiated. Types can implement an interface. Types that implement an interface are guaranteed to implement those fields of the interface.

```
interface Document{
  title: String
  text: String
  authors: [Author]
}
```

A regular type that implements the interface can extend the interface. In the following example, the type **Book** implements the interface **Document**.

```
type Book implements Document{
  id: ID!
}
```

The implementing type (**Book** in the example above) automatically contains the fields defined in the interface (**title**, **text**, and **authors** in the example above), they don't need to be mentioned explicitly. Additional fields can be defined in the type, such as the `id` field in the example above. To access the additional fields of a type implementing an interface in a query, we always need to make a distinction by type using inline fragments (see section 3.3.6).

## 2.9 Union

A *union* is a common type for several defining types. If an object is of a union type, it could be of any of its defining types. In the following, an object of type `Product` could be of type `Book` or of type `Software` or of type `Bread`.

```
union Product = Book|Software|Bread
```

So what is the difference between a union and an interface? The defining types of a union do not need to have any fields in common. With interfaces, however, the main purpose is to express common fields.

To access the fields of a union type in a query, we always need to make a distinction by type using the inline fragments (see section 3.3.6).

## 2.10 Input Types

*Input types* are used for passing input data in the form of arguments. Input types are used in mutations, when new objects are created or when objects are updated. When an instance of an input type is serialized, the data is formatted in JSON syntax.

The definition of input types looks exactly like the definition of regular object types, but with the keyword `input` instead of `type`. Note that input types cannot have fields of an object type, only scalar types, list types, and other input types. Despite the similar syntax, it is not possible to mix input types and regular types. To prevent mixing, it is a useful convention, to mark input types, e.g. by using the postfix `Input`.

```
input BookInput {
  title: String
  authors: [AuthorInput]
}
input AuthorInput {
      name: String
      books: [BookInput]
}
```

# 3 GraphQL Query Language

Clients use the GraphQL query language to interact with the GraphQL API.

How does this interaction work? The client first creates a GraphQL query using the GraphQL language and sends it to the API. The GraphQL API interprets the GraphQL query and responds with a JSON data structure.

What is a GraphQL query? A GraphQL query consists of one ore more patterns (see section 3.1) and one method (see section 2.4). The patterns are matched against parts of the graph. The method determines how the matched parts of the graph are processed. The language provides methods for retrieving data, writing data and getting notified when the data changes. For example with the query method, the matched parts of the graph are returned as results of the query.

## 3.1 Patterns

GraphQL queries consist of one or more patterns which are matched against the big graph containing all the data on the server. The patterns describe a subgraph of the big graph and is used to search for the relevant data in the big graph.

A pattern is expressed in terms of the relationships between objects and the fields the objects contain. This containment can be defined recursively. Let's have a look at an example of a pattern.

```
library {
  books {
```

```
        title
            id
    }
}
```

In the example, we see the pattern, which is used to search for a `library` object that contains `books` objects, which in turn contain both a `title` field and an `id` field. Curly brackets are used to express the containment. In front of the bracket is the name of the object (e.g. `library` or `books`), inside the brackets are the names of the fields of that object (e.g. `books` or `title` and `id`). Multi-level hierarchies can be built because a field can also be an object (e.g. `books`) which contains its own fields (e.g. `title` and `id`). When referring to several fields, they are each listed in a new line, without any separating commas or semicolons.

Speaking about semicolons: Note, that the GraphQL language is not JSON, even though it may look similar due to the use of angle brackets.

## 3.2 GraphQL Methods

Let's talk about the second ingredient of any GraphQL query besides the pattern: The GraphQL method. There are three methods in GraphQL:

- `query` is used for retrieval, for reading data (see section 3.3).

- `mutation` is used for modification, for writing data (see section 3.4).

- `subscription` is used for notification of changed data (see section 3.5).

In the following, we study each of the methods separately. These methods are represented by a type in the schema language.

26

## 3.3 GraphQL Query

To read data with GraphQL, the client uses the query method. In the pattern of this query, the client has to explicitly specify all the object and fields it is interested in. As a result of the query, the client gets exactly the objects and fields in the response that are specified in the request. Let's have a look at an example query.

```
query {
  books {
    title
  }
}
```

In this example, the client receives a list of books. Out of all the fields that book objects have, only the title will be returned for each book. Even though **books** might have other fields besides the **title**, these fields are not returned because they have not been explicitly requested in the query. Executing this query might result in the following data, which is returned in JSON format.

```
{
  "data": {
    "books": [
      {
        "title": "Book 1"
      },
      {
        "title": "Book 2"
      }
    ]
  }
}
```

What we first notice when using GraphQL for retrieval is that the structure of the response looks very similar to the query in the request. Query and response have the same shape. The query is comparable to a template in a template language. In the response, the client gets exactly the fields that are specified in the request, nothing additional, no surprises.

Just like functions in JavaScript, queries can be anonymous or named. Fopr simplicity, we have so far worked with anonymous queries. The advantages of named queries are similar to those of named functions. If the function is given a name, it allows us to identify it easier later on, e.g. for debugging or logging. In the following example, we give the query the name `myBookQuery`.

```
query myBookQuery{
  books {
    title
  }
}
```

### 3.3.1 Objects

Inside the query method, one or more objects can be retrieved. But an object cannot be retrieved without explicitly specifying the fields that should be returned. The object and its fields need to be described in the corresponding GraphQL schema (see chapter 2).

```
query {
  books {
    title
  }
}
```

In the example above, the `books` object and its `title` field are retrieved.

### 3.3.2 Fields

Listing the fields of an object in GraphQL corresponds to a `SELECT` in SQL. Each object, such as `books`, has one or more fields. The types of the fields are object, array or a primitive type. Objects have fields of their own, whereas primitives do not. Interestingly, the query language does not distinguish between lists and single elements, such as primitives or objects. If the field is a list (such as `books` in the example below), its fields (`title` in the example below) are actually the fields of each element in the list (each `book` in the list `books`).

28

We can include the fields of an object into the result, by explicitly listing each one of the fields that we want to include. In this example, we include the `title` field.

```
query {
  books {
    title
  }
}
```

It is also possible to retrieve multiple fields. In the following example, we request the title and `id` fields.

```
query {
  books {
    title
        id
  }
}
```

In the previous example, both the `title` and `id` fields had a primitive type. GraphQL becomes really interesting when the field has an object type instead of a primitive type. Then the object field has further fields itself, as demonstrated in the following example.

```
query {
  books {
    title
        author {
          name
        }
  }
}
```

In the above example, the `books` object has a field `author` of type `Author`. And since the type `Author` has the field `name`, we can ask for this field in the query. When a field of object type is included in the query, a new level of nesting is created for this field. In the resulting data, the result tree gets deeper, i.e. gets a new level.

### 3.3.3 Arguments

Some objects or fields may accept arguments. An argument is used to put constraints on objects. Only objects which satisfy the constraints imposed by the argument are included in the result. An argument in GraphQL is comparable to a `WHERE` clause in SQL.

In the following example, out of all the books in the graph, only the `book` with `id 1234` shall be included in the result set.

```
query {
  book_by_id(id:"1234"){
    title
  }
}
```

Arguments are listed in round brackets right behind the field or object name. The arguments are named (`id` in our example). In most programming languages, functions identify the arguments by the order they are passed, but not in GraphQL. In GraphQL the arguments are identified and passed by their name (`id` in our example).

### 3.3.4 Alias

When selecting multiple fields in a query, we may also want to select the same field more than once. This would result in a naming conflict, as there would be two fields with the same name in the result. To avoid the naming conflict, we can rename a field with an alias. Here we introduce the alias `second_book`.

```
query {
  book_by_id(id:"1234"){
    title
  }
  second_book: book_by_id(id:"5678"){
    title
  }
}
```

### 3.3.5 Fragments

Some queries contain repeating elements. In this case, it is tedious to get consistent in the first place and tedious to maintain consistency. Let's have a look at an example with repeating elements.

```
query {
  book_by_id(id:"1234"){
    title
    author {
      name
    }
  }
  second_book: book_by_id(id:"5678"){
    title
    author {
      name
    }
  }
}
```

Repeating elements of a query can be factored out into so-called fragments. Fragments need to be defined once (using the **fragment** keyword) and can be applied multiple times (using the ... keyword). Rewriting the example with fragments, results in the following.

```
query {
  book_by_id(id:"1234"){
    ...bookinfo
  }
  second_book: book_by_id(id:"5678"){
    ...bookinfo
  }
}

fragment bookinfo on Book{
  title
  author {
    name
  }
}
```

Note, that a fragment is defined for a specific type (see section 2.3), in our example, the fragment is specific for a **Book**.

### 3.3.6 Inline Fragments

Inline fragments are used to distinguish different types. It is similar to an **instanceof** operator in object-oriented programming languages. Inline fragments are for polymorphism, i.e. for **interface** (see 2.8) and **union** (see 2.9) types. It is not possible to statically determine all the fields available in an object, which implements the interface or union. This can only be accomplished at runtime with the use of the inline fragment. With

31

inline fragments we can check the type of an object at runtime
and deal with the fields of that particular object.

Let's illustrate this concept with an example. We have the
following type definitions in our schema (see chapter 2).

```
interface Document{
  title: String
  text: String
  authors: [Author]
}
type Book implements Document{
  id: ID!
}
type Article implements Document{
  magazine: String!
}
type Query{
  readingList: [Document]
}
```

The schema tells us that a Document can either be a Book
or an Article. Both Book and Article contain the fields of
Document, i.e. title, text and authors, but each type has
individual additional fields: a Book has an additional id field
and an Article has an additional magazine field. A Query has
a readingList of Documents.

How would a query for a readingList look like? Which fields
would we be able to access?

```
query{
  readingList{
    title
    text
    authors{
      name
    }
  }
}
```

With the above query, we can only access the fields which
are shared by all Documents, namely the fields title, text and
authors. We cannot access the specific fields of an Article or
Book in the readingList. This is because we would need to
distinguish the actual type of a Document. For this purpose, we
can use an inline fragment. In our example, we actually use two
inline fragments, one for Book and one for Article.

```
query{
  readingList{
    title
    text
    authors{
      name
    }
    ... on Book {
      id
    }
    ... on Article {
      magazine
    }
  }
}
```

As we have seen in the example above, inline fragments can
be used on interfaces (see section 2.8) to access additional fields
of implementing types. In union types (see section 2.9), inline
fragments are even more important. Since the member types of
a union in general share no fields, inline fragments have to be
used for accessing any field in a union.

### 3.3.7 Variables

Variables can be used to pass different values into a query. When
this value needs to be changed, the query itself can stay as it
is, since it only references the variable name. This allows for
reusing and validating the query, despite different values being
used. Often, variables are used for filtering, i.e. as GraphQL
arguments (see section 3.3.3). Let's have a look at an example
of a variable usage in a query

```
query getSpecificBook($bookID: String = "1234"){
  book_by_id(id: $bookID){
    title
  }
}
```

In the above example we filter for a book with a particular
id. The id is supplied in the variable $bookID. Variables are de-
clared right after the query keyword and the name of the query.
Variables have the scope of the complete query. Variables need
to have a type (primitive or object type). Moreover, variables

may have a default value. When no value is passed to the variable explicitly, it will have the value of the default value. In the above example a default value is specified for the variable $bookID and its value is ``1234''.

### 3.3.8 Directives

*Directives* can be used to dynamically include or exclude a part of a query. Dynamically means depending on the value of a boolean variable (see section 3.3.7 on variables); this boolean variable has to be declared just like any other variable. Directives are modelled as annotations in a query and can be attached to a **field** or a **fragment**. There are two types of directives: one to include (**@include** keyword) a part of the query and one to exclude (**@skip** keyword) a part of the query.

```
query getBooks($flag: boolean){
  books{
    title
        id @include(if: $flag)
  }
}
```

The above example includes the id field only if the value of $flag is true.

```
query getBooks($flag: boolean){
  books{
    title
        id @skip(if: $flag)
  }
}
```

The above example is similar to the first one, but the logic is reversed. It skips the id field if $flag is true, meaning it includes the id field only if the value of $flag is false.

## 3.4 GraphQL Mutation

Just as the **query** method is used for reading data, the **mutation** method is used for modifying, adding or writing data on the server with GraphQL. Let's have a look at an example of a typical mutation.

```
mutation {
  addBook(title: "New Book"){
    id
    title
  }
}
```

The above mutation creates a book object with title ``New Book'' and adds it to the graph. The values for the fields of the newly created object are passed as arguments. Arguments are named and are identified based on their name - not based on their position in the argument list, as it is typical for programming languages.

After adding the book, the mutation returns the newly created book object. However, it does not return the complete book object with all its attributes, but only the explicitly listed attributes of the new book: id and title in the example.

## 3.5 GraphQL Subscription

Modern clients need to get near real-time updates that get triggered when something changes on the server. For example, an instant messaging app needs to get notified, when a new message arrives on the server, or a weather app needs to get notified when a weather warning gets published.

REST does not provide any built-in support for such notifications from the server; thus notifications are often realized by polling or by webhooks. Learn more about webhooks and polling in this book [4].

- With polling, the client periodically sends requests to the server, to check if any new data is available. The client usually needs to poll on an endpoint that returns a list of elements and compares the retrieved list against the previously retrieved list in order to find the new elements.

Polling is expensive for both client and server, as it binds a lot of resources.

- With webhooks, the server calls the client, whenever new data becomes available. To set this up, the client first needs to register an endpoint that gets called by the server when a certain type of event happens. In order to receive events, the client needs to be able to expose an endpoint that can receive the events.

GraphQL offers subscriptions as a built-in mechanism for realizing notifications. After the client has subscribed to an event, it gets notified by the server when new events occur.

The first step of using GraphQL subscriptions is for the client to send a subscription request to the GraphQL API. The request specifies both the event (`bookAdded` in the example) to observe and the data (`id` and `title` of the newly added book), which should be sent from the server to the client, when the event is actually triggered.

```
subscription {
  bookAdded {
    id
    title
  }
}
```

What triggers a notification? In most cases, a notification is triggered by a modification of the data inside the graph, i.e. by a mutation. This means that an event handler needs to be installed inside the implementation of the mutation. In rare cases, a notification could be triggered by an external event, which is not directly accessible inside the graph or only accessible in aggregated form. An example is sensor data, of which a single measurement may be used as a trigger, whereas the graph only contains aggregated sensor data and no single measurements.

# 4 Building A GraphQL API

In this chapter, we discuss the features of a GraphQL API and the mechanics behind it (see section 4.1), the architecture of a GraphQL server (see section 4.2) and the design methodology for GraphQL APIs (see section 4.3)

## 4.1 GraphQL API Mechanics

All GraphQL APIs offer a number of features that we need to understand in order to build GraphQL APIs. This section teaches the mechanics behind the GraphQL features. These features are typically provided by a GraphQL runtime system and GraphQL libraries. They do not have to be coded by each API developer. However, to be able to use this predefined functionality, the libraries have to be used and configured correctly. The heart of this configuration is the GraphQL schema with its type definitions.

### 4.1.1 GraphQL Validation

Any request that is received by a GraphQL API, is first syntactically validated against the GraphQL schema. The correct usage of types, fields, arguments and other language elements is checked. In case of a validation error, a description of the error is sent back to the client. The GraphQL runtime (see section 1.2.3) typically takes on the task of request validation. The creator of the GraphQL API only needs to provide the schema.

## 4.1.2 GraphQL Execution

After the request has been validated, it needs to be interpreted and executed by the server to create a response. For the execution of the request, the GraphQL server can rely on the type system provided by the schema. The schema provides the syntax, but also - at least on the top level - the semantics of a GraphQL query. The operational semantics of the schema is provided by the resolver function (see section 4.1.2.2)

At the top level of every GraphQL schema is a type that represents all of the possible entry points into the GraphQL API, it's often called the root type or the method (see section 2.4). The execution semantics depends on the method that is executed: query (see section 4.1.2.1), mutation (see section 4.1.2.3) or subscription (see section 4.1.2.4).

### 4.1.2.1 Execution of Queries

After being validated, a GraphQL query is executed by a GraphQL server. The GraphQL server returns a result that structurally mirrors the shape of the requested query. Before being sent to the client, the server serializes the result, typically in JSON format.

Creating a response to a query is actually a traversal of the graph. This traversal is also called resolution and is described below. While the data on the server forms a graph structure, the query produces a forest data structure as a result. A forest data structure consists of one or more tree data structures. All trees of the result forest are collected in a data object. This data object forms the root of the response, which is typically serialized in JSON. The shape of the result mirrors the shape of the query. GraphQL queries are processed immediately and in parallel with other queries.

The actual processing happens in the resolver function, which we discuss in the next section. It is the task of the GraphQL API developer to provide the resolver function.

### 4.1.2.2 Resolver Functions

The resolver function defines the operational semantics -- or behavior – of the types and fields in the schema. Each type defined in the schema needs to be backed by a resolver function. As input, the resolver function takes basically the data, which is a subgraph of the big GraphQL graph. As output, the resolver function produces either a list of matched subgraphs or a list of scalar values. Initially, the argument of the resolver function is the complete graph.

For execution, the resolver function is called recursively i.e. for each of the subgraphs produced as output. A subgraph is an instance of a certain type. When such a subgraph is processed, the resolver function of its corresponding type is called. If the resolver function for a certain subgraph produces a scalar value like a string or number, then the recursion terminates in that branch. If the resolver function for a certain subgraph produces another subgraph, the resolver function is called for each subgraph. This continues until all subgraphs are resolved to scalar values. A resolver function typically accesses a database and then constructs a response based on the result of the database query.

Previously I stated that the resolver function takes the subgraph as input. This is actually a simplification. In fact, a resolver function receives three arguments:

- `obj`: the parent object of the field being resolved (for a field of the `Query/Mutation/Subscription` type, obj is often `null` or left out).

- `args`: the arguments (see section 3.3.3) provided to the field in the GraphQL query/mutation/subscription.

- `context`: holds important contextual information, such as the authenticated user and access to a database.

### 4.1.2.3 Execution of Mutations

Executing a mutation and creating a response entails a modification of the graph. Modification may mean changing existing nodes and relations or adding new nodes and relations to the graph. In addition, the new or modified node is returned.

Mutations need to be processed sequentially to prevent race conditions. Thus, mutations are put into a queue in the order they are received. If a mutation is fired before the previous mutation has finished processing, the second mutation is put into a queue, where it waits until the first one has finished. Only then it is scheduled for processing.

Conceptually, queries are used for reading data and mutations are used for writing data. However, there is no enforcement of this rule, we could write data in a query. The only difference between mutations and queries is that queries are executed immediately and in parallel, whereas mutations are executed sequentially, in the order given. Mutation number two has to wait until mutation number one has finished.

### 4.1.2.4 Execution of Subscriptions

Handling a subscription entails registering the client for the chosen event. There is no confirmation response. A response is only generated when the event actually occurs. GraphQL does not prescribe any technology binding. It is, however, best practice to realize this bidirectional communication via the WebSocket protocol.

### 4.1.3 GraphQL Introspection

GraphQL offers an introspection feature, based on the type definitions. Introspection allows us to ask GraphQL for any information that is part of the user-defined schema at runtime.

The introspection feature does not have to be implemented by the API developer. It is provided automatically by the GraphQL runtime. The only thing that needs to be provided by the GraphQL developer are the type definitions in the schema.

There are special keywords for requesting meta information. They start with __, such as __schema or __type or __field. Here is a sample request listing all the types available, including built-in types, meta types, user-defined types and scalar types.

```
{
  __schema{
    types{
      name
    }
  }
}
```

To interact with the introspection system, no special tool is required, any GraphQL client that can execute queries, can also use the introspection capabilities.

### 4.1.4 GraphiQL

GraphiQL is a GraphQL client, which provides a simple user interface of the GraphQL API. GraphiQL is realized as a web application, and in practice it is often hosted on the same server that runs the GraphQL API. GraphiQL is targeted at the developers of the GraphQL API and at developers building applications with the GraphQL API. It provides great support for developing GraphQL queries for clients, for testing the implementation of the GraphQL API or for a quick and simple demo of the API.

The GraphiQL tool offers syntax-directed editing, syntax highlighting and auto completion, since it is enabled by GraphQL

41

introspection (see section 4.1.3). It can be used as part of an API portal where it may serve as an interactive documentation and an API discovery and exploration tool. The documentation displayed in GraphiQL is guaranteed to be consistent with the implementation, since it is based on the same schema as the implementation.

## 4.1.5 GraphQL Libraries

When building a GraphQL server implementation we should use a library. Libraries are available for all major programming languages. In the tutorial of this book (see chapter 5) we use node.js to implement our GraphQL API with the Apollo express-graphql.

But libraries are not only available for building GraphQL APIs on the server side. There are also a number of GraphQL client libraries available. GraphQL is popular among frontend developers, who are creating clients. There are many reasons for this, e.g. since GraphQL has a low latency and fewer roundtrips. It is easy to find the documentation, and it is possible to use introspection for figuring out, what data is served by the endpoint. All these features are typically valued by API clients. There are also a number of convenient client libraries that make it even more convenient to work with GraphQL APIs for the client. These libraries may, for example, help the client developer to create and execute GraphQL queries. They help with a client-side cache management to ensure that all GraphQL results are consistent with one another and to update the cache with results from the server when using e.g. mutations, pagination and subscriptions. Client libraries are not only available for React and JavaScript, but also for example for Ruby, Java, .net, Python, Go and Scalar.

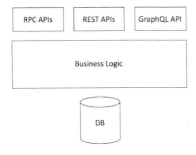

Figure 4.1: Greenfield API Architecture

## 4.2 GraphQL Server Architecture

The GraphQL server is typically realized as a 3-tier architecture, consisting of a front-facing layer, a business-logic layer and a database layer (see Figure 4.1). The GraphQL API is used as a front-facing layer, just as REST, RPC or SOAP are used as front-facing layers.

Typically, only one front-facing layer is required. But one might want to exchange the front-facing layer or build several alternative front-facing layers in parallel.

The advantage of this 3-layer architecture is, that GraphQL can reuse the same basic business logic that a REST API, RPC API or SOAP API could use. This would also make it possible to provide e.g. both a GraphQL API and a REST API, while being cost-efficient through maximum reuse of the business-logic layer. To make this approach work, it is key to implement basic business functionality in the business-logic layer independently of the front-facing architectural style chosen for the API.

43

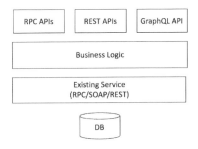

Figure 4.2: Legacy API Architecture

## 4.2.1 Greenfield Case

When a new GraphQL API is built without involving any existing legacy systems, we call this a greenfield case. Sometimes we have the luxury of building a greenfield API, all the way to the backend and database. In this case, we would realize a three tier architecture with a database for persistence, a business layer, which creates business objects based on the data and a presentation layer, which prepares the data for presentation in a front-facing layer (see Figure 4.1).

## 4.2.2 Legacy Case

In enterprises, we usually do not have the luxury of starting fresh and designing the system from the ground up, as we do in the greenfield case. Instead, we need to deal with existing legacy services and databases. Those usually do not have the optimal structure, so we need to decouple the new front-facing layer by a new business logic layer from the existing legacy services (see Figure 4.2).

## 4.3 GraphQL API Design Methodology

### 4.3.1 API Design Approach

The fundamental idea is to design APIs as a digital product in its own right. Being a digital product, the API needs to be consumer-oriented. Now what does that mean and who are the consumers of an API?

#### 4.3.1.1 Consumer-Oriented API Design

The consumers of an API are the various developers building clients with the API. And the essence of consumer-orientation is knowing the consumers including their needs and desires and putting these needs and desires of the API consumers first when designing the API. We need to know our prototypical API consumers, their needs, and the architecture of the solutions they are building. Our API should be as simple, clean, clear and approachable as possible from their perspective, i.e. from the perspective of the prototypical API consumers. It is important to stress this aspect since internal constraints and legacy systems otherwise tend to dominate API design.

#### 4.3.1.2 Reusability

Consumer-oriented design can sometimes lead into the trap of basically designing an API for one customer only, i.e. designing for the very narrow needs of one consumer only. Instead, APIs need to be reusable products that can be reused by various consumers and in various use cases.

Despite being consumer-oriented, a product also needs to be somewhat generic, so it can be used by a wide range of customers. The API needs to be reusable in various solutions.

### 4.3.1.3 API Product Design

The basic process for GraphQL API design is no different than the basic process for API design of REST APIs [3]. If we design APIs as reusable products and design them from the perspective of the prototypical API consumers, then we are on the way to build consumer-oriented APIs – APIs that our consumers will love.

## 4.3.2 GraphQL API Design Phases

Let's start with an overview of the phases in this API design approach. Each phase of this approach consists of a creative part, and a verification part. During the creative part an artifact is crafted, during the verification part early feedback on the artifact is collected. In each phase of the design and development journey, feedback from the consumers is elicited. It is important to collect the feedback as early as possible, when changes to the API are still possible, relatively simple and can be implemented with low risk, low effort, and low costs.

This design approach is meant to be used iteratively. There are small iterations which are triggered by the verification part of the same phase. And there are also big iterations, which are triggered by one of the later verification phases and require going back to the creative part of an earlier phase. Keep in mind, that in an iterative and agile approach, not all information and requirements about the constructed artifact need to be available in the beginning, but new and more detailed information and insights are gathered and integrated during each iteration. We need to get feedback from customers on the API design and build the GraphQL API outside-in. This means we need to start from the needs of the API consumer towards the existing legacy systems. And not the other way!

Our proposed API design approach is organized in six phases.

### 4.3.2.1 Phase 1: Domain Analysis

Domain analysis should get us thinking from an API consumer perspective: Who are the consumers of the API? What is the purpose of the API? Which API solutions do the consumers plan to build with the API? Which other API solutions would be possible with the API? How does an API consumer prefer to interact with the data delivered by the API?

### 4.3.2.2 Phase 2: Architectural Design

In the architectural design phase, we choose a server architecture (see section 4.2), an API philosophy, and an architectural style for realizing the API. In the scope of this book, let's assume we choose a three-level server architecture with GraphQL as our API philosophy in the front-facing layer.

### 4.3.2.3 Phase 3: Prototyping

For prototyping a GraphQL API we need to define a schema (see chapter 2), which contains all the relevant types in the type graph. We use automatically created mock data, to simulate the response of the API and get some first feedback on the API design. In this phase we can iterate multiple times by extending the schema and collecting feedback based on the mocked API.

### 4.3.2.4 Phase 4: Implementing for Production

When implementing for production, we gradually move away from the use of mocked data, towards real data and real back-end systems. At this point, the accidental complexity of the organically grown legacy systems may hit us and the API developers. In the implementation phase, non-functional properties come into focus, such as stability, performance, and security.

### 4.3.2.5 Phase 5: Publishing

As soon as the GraphQL API is published, it needs to stay backward compatible with the originally published version. Only backward compatible changes are possible. Knowing about this hard cut imposed with initial publication of the GraphQL API, we need to ask if we have tested enough and have received enough consumer feedback to be confident to take the big leap of publishing the API.

### 4.3.2.6 Phase 6: Maintenance

During the maintenance phase, bugs and issues may be resolved, but also new functionality may be introduced, as long as it is backward compatible: functionality and fields may be added without breaking clients, but removing functionality or fields is not permitted.

Further down the line, we want to learn whether and why consumers use the API. We need to observe the metrics of our API to learn how consumers use the API. This cannot be based on analytics alone, but we need to communicate with our API consumers one-on-one and build and active community.

# 5 GraphQL API Tutorial

The goal of this tutorial is to write our first GraphQL API with Node.js and the Apollo GraphQL library. Step by step we build an API and extend its functionality. The GraphQL API we build in this tutorial serves a list of books. Each book has a title, an id and a list of authors, and each author has a name and an id. By the end we will have built a GraphQL API, serving information about books and authors, supporting different queries, a mutation, and a subscription.

This tutorial is organized in 6 steps:

- We start out with the setup and some preparations for working with GraphQL (see step 0 in section 5.1).

- We build a first simple GraphQL API with a schema, an HTTP server and automatically created mock data, which can already process a GraphQL query (see step 1 in section 5.2).

- We extend this API by replacing the mocked data with "real" data and a GraphQL resolver (see step 2 in section 5.3).

- We create a second query with arguments and extend the resolver function (see step 3 in section 5.4).

- So far the API has two different queries for reading data; we add writing data to the API by adding support for a mutation (see step 4 in section 5.5).

- We then add support for subscriptions and notification, so the server can send data to the client when triggered by an event (see step 5 in section 5.6).

Each step extends the solution built in the previous step, so by the end of the tutorial we will have built a complete GraphQL API. It is possible to jump over some steps, we just need to download the prepared source code: the solution for each step (see section 5.1.2) is offered as a download.

# 5.1 Step 0 - Preparations

Before we can write our first GraphQL API, we need to setup and download a number of things. The information in this section helps with these preparations.

### 5.1.1 Install Node and Node Package Manager

Let's download and install Node.js from https://nodejs.org. Afterwards we can test, whether Node.js is properly installed by entering the following commands on the command line.

```
> node -v
v8.2.1
> npm -v
5.3.0
```

Both commands should return a version number and, of course, it does not have to be the same as shown here for illustration purposes.

### 5.1.2 Download the Tutorial Solutions

The provided zip file contains the source code files for each of the following 5 tutorial steps. For each step (1-5) of this tutorial, the following source code files are available:

- `schema.js`: The GraphQL schema definition

50

- `resolvers.js`: The source code for resolving GraphQL requests.

- `server.js`: The HTTP and WS (Websockets) server, which realizes the GraphQL binding.

- `package.json`: The meta information, including dependencies and start script.

---

Download the Tutorial Solutions:

https://api-university.com/books/graphql-api-design/tutorial

---

### 5.1.3 Install Tutorial Dependencies

The download package only contains the source code. It does not contain the libraries that are required as external dependencies. The dependencies need to be downloaded and installed separately. It is recommended to download and install the dependencies with the node package manager tool **npm** (it should be part of the Node.js installation, see section 5.1.1). To use it, let's first open a command line and navigate to the directory with our tutorial files, then use the following command (all in one line) to download and install all the necessary dependencies:

```
npm install -save graphql express graphql-server-express body-parser
graphql-tools graphql-subscriptions subscriptions-transport-ws
```

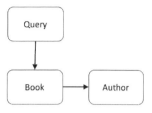

Figure 5.1: Example Type Graph

# 5.2 Step 1 - Initial API with Mocked Data

The GraphQL API we build in this tutorial is supposed to be used to manage the books in a library. We can retrieve a list of books from the API. Each book has a title, an id and a list of authors. Authors have a name and an id.

In this first step, we build a simple GraphQL API with a schema (see section 5.2.1), and bind it to an HTTP server (see section 5.2.2). The API can process a GraphQL query, which returns a list of books. Initially, this list of books is based on automatically created mock data.

## 5.2.1 Schema

We start with a domain analysis and first model the types graphically, as shown in section 2.1. This results in figure 5.1.

Based on the graphical representation of the types and the relationships between the types, we create a GraphQL type definition, expressed using the GraphQL Schema Language (see chapter 2).

```
type Book {
  id: ID!
  title: String
  authors: [Author]
}
type Author {
    id: ID!
    name: String
```

```
}
type Query {
  books: [Book]
}
```

This type definition is a central part of the GraphQL API implementation, it is a part of the source code in `schema.js`. Now, let's have a look at the source code in `schema.js`:

```
var {makeExecutableSchema,addMockFunctionsToSchema} = require('graphql-tools');
const typeDefs = `
type Book {
      id: ID!
      title: String
      authors: [Author]
}
type Author {
      id: ID!
      name: String
}
type Query {
      books: [Book]
}
`;
var schema = makeExecutableSchema({ typeDefs });
addMockFunctionsToSchema({ schema });
module.exports = schema;
```

What can we see in this source code? The type definition is included verbatim (note the special quotation marks for multi-line strings) in the string variable `typeDefs`. The type definition is made executable by the `makeExecutableSchema` function, provided by the library `graphql-tools`. The function takes a type definition string and turns it into an executable schema for our server to use. Think of an executable schema as a form of parser. We also let GraphQL create mocked data by the `addMockFunctionsToSchema` function, provided by the library `graphql-tools`.

## 5.2.2 Server

The source code in `server.js` binds the GraphQL schema (created in section 5.2.1) to an HTTP endpoint.

```
var express = require('express');
var {graphqlExpress,graphiqlExpress} = require('graphql-server-express');
var bodyParser = require('body-parser');
var schema = require('./schema.js');
```

53

```
const PORT = 4000;
const server = express();

server.get('/', function (req, res) {  res.send('Hello World!');});
server.listen(PORT, () => console.log(`GraphQL on port ${PORT}`));
server.use('/graphql', bodyParser.json(), graphqlExpress({ schema }));
server.use('/graphiql', graphiqlExpress({ endpointURL: '/graphql' }));
```

The above code makes use of a lot of different libraries, such as the Node.js HTTP server of the library **express**, and the JSON parser of the library **body-parser**. It also uses a generic GraphQL server implementation that can be stacked on top of express (**graphqlExpress**) and the generic implementation of the GraphiQL user interface, which is also stacked on top of express (**graphiqlExpress**).

In the **server.js** code, these components are wired up and connected with the **schema.js** implementation, created in section 5.2.1.

After the server is started, the express server is listening on port 4000 with handlers for the paths **/graphql** and **/graphiql**. When the path **/graphql** is requested, a JSON structure is expected and parsed. It is then routed to the **graphqlExpress** function, which uses the executable GraphQL schema. It interprets the query. When the path **/graphiql** is called, the request is routed to the **graphiqlExpress** function, which makes use of the previously defined **/graphql** endpoint. It delivers the GraphiQL web application.

### 5.2.3 Running the Tutorial API

To run the API, open a command line and navigate to the directory with our tutorial files of the respective step (e.g. **cd graphql-tutorial/step1**), then use the command

```
npm start
```

If everything is set up correctly, we will see the message

```
GraphQL Server is now running on http://localhost:4000
```

54

## 5.2.4 Testing the Tutorial API

After having started the tutorial API (see section 5.2.3), let's test the API with a GraphQL client. For this purpose, we use the tool GraphiQL. It is a user interface for GraphQL APIs and allows executing GraphQL methods and inspecting their responses. GraphiQL uses GraphQL introspection for displaying documentation and providing a type-safe playground. GraphiQL is a web application, which – in our case – is served by the same HTTP server that serves the API. To access GraphiQL, let's open the following URL in our browser:

```
http://localhost:4000/graphiql
```

Enter the request shown in section 5.2.4.1 on the left side and press the play button. Does the API answer with the expected response shown in section 5.2.4.2?

### 5.2.4.1 Request

```
query {
  books{
    id
    title
    authors{
      name
    }
  }
}
```

### 5.2.4.2 Response

```
{
  "data": {
    "books": [
      {
        "id": "a443cc47-17ea-49aa-ac39-129d8d5d0ba1",
        "title": "Hello World",
        "authors": [
          {
            "name": "Hello World"
          },{
            "name": "Hello World"
          }
        ]
```

55

```
    },
    {
      "id": "f46a5213-a85f-414d-8d42-baae07fde7c5",
      "title": "Hello World",
      "authors": [
        {
          "name": "Hello World"
        },
        {
          "name": "Hello World"
        }
      ]
    }
  ]
}
}
```

Where does this response data come from? The data we see was generated by the GraphQL mock data generator that creates type-conform mock data. For IDs, it generates random UUIDs and for Strings, it sets the static value `` `Hello World'' ``.

# 5.3 Step 2 - Add a Resolver and Real Data

In step 1 our GraphQL API served automatically generated mock data. In step 2 we will change this and connect the GraphQL API to some "real" data. To avoid the overhead of adding support for a particular database, the backend data is hardcoded. It should be straightforward to get the data from the database instead of the hardcoded values. We continue to work on the source code that we have created in the previous step.

## 5.3.1 Resolvers

To deal with real data, a new file `resolvers.js` is created. Resolvers map GraphQL queries to result data. Let's have a look at one such resolver.

```
var resolvers = {
    Query: {
        books: () => {
            return books;
        },
    },
```

```
};
module.exports = resolvers;
```

The above resolver accepts a query for **books** without parameters and returns a **books** object. When we add the hardcoded data, this results in the following contents of **resolvers.js**:

```
var authors = [{
        id: 1,
        name: 'Author 1'
  },{
        id: 2,
        name: 'Author 2'
  }
];
var books = [{
        id: 3,
        title: 'Book 1',
        authors: [authors[0]]
  },{
        id: 4,
        title: 'Book 2',
        authors: [authors[0],authors[1]]
  }
];
var resolvers = {
        Query: {
                books: () => {
                        return books;
                },
        },
};
module.exports = resolvers;
```

## 5.3.2 Schema

We need to modify the source code of **schema.js** created in the previous step. Mocked data is no longer required, so we remove **addMockFunctionsToSchema()**. To make our server use the **resolvers()** function we just defined, we have to import it in **schema.js** and pass it to the function **makeExecutableSchema()**, as shown below.

```
var {makeExecutableSchema,addMockFunctionsToSchema} = require('graphql-tools');
var resolvers = require('./resolvers.js');
const typeDefs = `
  type Book {
    id: ID!
        title: String
        authors: [Author]
  }
  type Author {
        id: ID!
```

```
        name: String
    }
    type Query {
        books: [Book]
    }
`;
var schema = makeExecutableSchema({ typeDefs, resolvers });
module.exports = schema;
```

### 5.3.3 Server

The source code in `server.js` that was created in step 1, is not affected by this change and does not need to be changed.

### 5.3.4 Testing

To test whether our server is working, let's open the URL `http://localhost:4000/graphiql` in the browser and send the request shown in section 5.3.4.1. Does the response of the API match with the expected response shown in section 5.3.4.2?

#### 5.3.4.1 Request

```
query {
  books{
    id
    title
    authors{
      name
    }
  }
}
```

#### 5.3.4.2 Response

```
{
  "data": {
    "books": [
      {
        "id": "3",
        "title": "Book 1",
        "authors": [
          {
            "name": "Author 1"
          }
        ]
```

```
    },
    {
      "id": "4",
      "title": "Book 2",
      "authors": [
        {
          "name": "Author 1"
        },
        {
          "name": "Author 2"
        }
      ]
    }
  ]
 }
}
```

## 5.4 Step 3 - Query with Arguments

In step 3 we add support for querying the graph for a specific
book, identified by its title. We realize this new functionality
by an additional query. The new query is realized by a resolver
function, which takes the title of the book as an argument. Here
is an example of such a request.

```
query {
  book(title: "Book 1"){
    id
  }
}
```

### 5.4.1 Schema

To support the new query, we need to change the type definitions
in schema.js. We add:

```
book(title:String!): Book
```

This results in the following schema.js

```
var {makeExecutableSchema,addMockFunctionsToSchema} = require('graphql-tools');
var resolvers = require('./resolvers.js');
const typeDefs = `
  type Book {
    id: ID!
    title: String
    authors: [Author]
  }
  type Author {
```

```
  id: ID!
  name: String
}
type Query {
  books: [Book]
  book(title:String!): Book
}
`;
var schema = makeExecutableSchema({ typeDefs, resolvers });
module.exports = schema;
```

## 5.4.2 Resolvers

To handle the new query type, a corresponding resolver function for `book()` needs to be added in `resolvers.js`. A resolver function receives three arguments:

- `obj`: the parent object of the field being resolved

- `args`: the arguments (see section 3.3.3) provided to the field in the GraphQL query/mutation/subscription

- `context`: holds important contextual information, such as the authenticated user and access to a database

In the resolver function for `book`, the `obj` parameter is the `root` object (but it is not used inside the resolver), `args` are passed and the `context` is not required. The resolver function filters the appropriate book out of the complete book list. In the scope of this tutorial, the complete book list is just a static, hardcoded array. In a real implementation, one would get the book list from a database, and let the database engine perform the search efficiently.

```
book: (root, args) => {
    var res=null;
    books.forEach(function(b){
        if (b.title === args.title) res=b;
    });
    return res;
},
```

Integrating the new resolver into `resolvers.js` results in:

```
var authors = [{
        id: 1,
        name: 'Author 1'
  },{
        id: 2,
        name: 'Author 2'
  }
];
var books = [{
        id: 3,
        title: 'Book 1',
        authors: [authors[0]]
  },{
        id: 4,
        title: 'Book 2',
        authors: [authors[0],authors[1]]
  }
];
var resolvers = {
        Query: {
                books: () => {
                        return books;
                },
                book: (root, args) => {
                        var res=null;
                        books.forEach(function(b){
                                if (b.title === args.title) res=b;
                        });
                        return res;
                },
        },
};
module.exports = resolvers;
```

## 5.4.3 Testing

To test whether our server is working, let's open the URL
http://localhost:4000/graphiql in the browser and send the
request from section 5.4.3.1. Does the response of the API match
the response shown in section 5.4.3.2?

### 5.4.3.1 Request

```
query {
  book(title: "Book 1"){
    id
    title
    authors{
      name
    }
  }
}
```

61

### 5.4.3.2 Response

```
{
  "data": {
    "book": {
      "id": "3",
      "title": "Book 1",
      "authors": [
        {
          "name": "Author 1"
        }
      ]
    }
  }
}
```

# 5.5 Step 4 - Mutation

In step 4 we extend the functionality of the API to add a specific book to the graph. In GraphQL, such a writing functionality is realized by a mutation. With the following mutation request, it should be possible to add the book with the title "The New Book" to the graph and return the newly generated id of the book.

```
mutation{
  addBook(title: "The New Book"){
    id
  }
}
```

## 5.5.1 Schema

A mutation is represented by a type. In the type definition of the schema, we add a new type for mutation, called addBook, which takes the title of the book as an obligatory (note the !) argument.

```
type Mutation {
    addBook(title: String!): Book
}
```

Integrating the mutation into the existing schema.js file results in:

62

```
var {makeExecutableSchema,addMockFunctionsToSchema} = require('graphql-tools');
var resolvers = require('./resolvers.js');
const typeDefs = `
  type Book {
    id: ID!
    title: String
    authors: [Author]
  }
  type Author {
    id: ID!
    name: String
  }
  type Query {
    books: [Book]
    book(title:String!): Book
  }
  type Mutation {
    addBook(title: String!): Book
  }
`;
var schema = makeExecutableSchema({ typeDefs, resolvers });
module.exports = schema;
```

## 5.5.2 Resolvers

A new handler needs to be added for the mutation type in
resolvers.js. The resolver constructs a newBook object, by
using the title received as argument from the request and by
creating a unique id based on an instance counter (nextId).
The newly created book is added to the list books and finally,
the newly created book is returned.

```
Mutation: {
    addBook: (root, args) => {
        var newBook = {id: nextId++, title: args.title };
        books.push(newBook);
        return newBook;
    },
}
```

The instance counter (nextId) needs to be defined as a global
variable.

```
var nextId = 5;
```

All changes add up to the following contents of resolvers.js:

```
var authors = [{
    id: 1,
    name: 'Author 1'
},{
    id: 2,
```

63

```
            name: 'Author 2'
    }
];
var books = [{
        id: 3,
        title: 'Book 1',
        authors: [authors[0]]
    },{
        id: 4,
        title: 'Book 2',
        authors: [authors[0],authors[1]]
    }
];
var nextId = 5;
var resolvers = {
        Query: {
                books: () => {
                        return books;
                },
                book: (root, args) => {
                        var res = null;
                        books.forEach(function(b){
                                if (b.title === args.title) res=b;
                        });
                        return res;
                },
        },
        Mutation: {
                addBook: (root, args) => {
                        var newBook = {id: nextId++, title: args.title };
                        books.push(newBook);
                        return newBook;
                },
        }
};
module.exports = resolvers;
```

## 5.5.3 Testing

To test whether our server is working, let's open the address
http://localhost:4000/graphiql in the browser and send the
request shown in section 5.5.3.1. Does the response of the API
match the response shown in section 5.5.3.2? Let's send a second
request to retrieve the list of books and check if the effect of the
mutation is visible. Does the response of the API match with
the response shown in section 5.5.3.4, when sending the query
shown in section 5.5.3.3?

### 5.5.3.1 Mutation Request

```
mutation{
  addBook(title: "The New Book"){
    id
    title
  }
}
```

## 5.5.3.2 Mutation Response

```
{
  "data": {
    "addBook": {
      "id": "5",
      "title": "The New Book"
    }
  }
}
```

## 5.5.3.3 Query Request

To check for the effect of the mutation, we perform a second
request. This request is supposed to return the id and title of
each book.

```
query {
  books{
    id
    title
  }
}
```

## 5.5.3.4 Query Response

```
{
  "data": {
    "books": [
      {
        "id": "3",
        "title": "Book 1"
      },
      {
        "id": "4",
        "title": "Book 2"
      },
      {
        "id": "5",
        "title": "The New Book"
      }
    ]
```

```
    }
}
```

# 5.6 Step 5 - Subscription

In step 5 we add a subscription, which should (1) allow clients to
register for event notification and (2) actually send out an event
notification to registered clients when a new book is added.

## 5.6.1 Schema

We add the built-in `Subscription` type to our schema, which
has a `bookAdded` field of type `Book`. The `bookAdded` field represents a topic, a type of event that can be subscribed to.

```
type Subscription {
        bookAdded: Book
}
```

This results in the following source code for `schema.js`:

```
var {makeExecutableSchema,addMockFunctionsToSchema} = require('graphql-tools');
var resolvers = require('./resolvers.js');
const typeDefs = `
  type Book {
    id: ID!
    title: String
    authors: [Author]
  }
  type Author {
    id: ID!
    name: String
  }
  type Query {
    books: [Book]
    book(title:String!): Book
  }
  type Mutation {
    addBook(title: String!): Book
  }
  type Subscription {
    bookAdded: Book
  }
`;
var schema = makeExecutableSchema({ typeDefs, resolvers });
module.exports = schema;
```

## 5.6.2 Resolvers

To implement GraphQL Subscriptions we have to implement two tasks: (1) subscribing a client to a certain topic and (2) delivering event notifications to the subscribed clients.

The GraphQL library `graphql-subscriptions` offers support for implementing those two tasks, by providing the PubSub class. It allows us to manage a list of subscribers for several topics and send out an event to all subscribed clients.

```
var {PubSub} = require('graphql-subscriptions');
var pubsub = new PubSub();
```

### 5.6.2.1 Subscribing a Client

We allow clients to register or subscribe to the event with the `bookAdded` function. The clients will be subscribed only to events with the topic `bookAddedTopic`. The topic is only visible internally in our implementation and never communicated to a client.

```
Subscription: {
        bookAdded: {
                subscribe: () => pubsub.asyncIterator('bookAddedTopic')
        }
}
```

### 5.6.2.2 Delivering Event Notifications

We deliver events by adding a notification trigger in the mutation processing. We publish an event, whenever a new book is added by a mutation. We use the PubSub object to publish the event to all registered clients. The event contains a type or topic (here: `bookAddedTopic`) and the newly created book.

```
pubsub.publish('bookAddedTopic', {bookAdded: newBook});
```

### 5.6.2.3 Complete Resolver

The changes described above add up to the following `resolvers.js`

```
var {PubSub} = require('graphql-subscriptions');
var pubsub = new PubSub();
var authors = [{
        id: 1,
        name: 'Author 1'
    },{
        id: 2,
        name: 'Author 2'
    }
];
var books = [{
        id: 1,
        title: 'Book 1',
        authors: [authors[0]]
    },{
        id: 2,
        title: 'Book 2',
        authors: [authors[0],authors[1]]
    }
];
var nextId = 5;
var resolvers = {
        Query: {
                books: () => {
                        return books;
                },
                book: (root, args) => {
                        var res = null;
                        books.forEach(function(b){
                                if (b.title === args.title) res=b;
                        });
                        return res;
                },
        },
        Mutation: {
                addBook: (root, args) => {
                        var newBook = {id: nextId++, title: args.title };
                        books.push(newBook);
                        pubsub.publish('bookAddedTopic', { bookAdded: newBook});
                        return newBook;
                },
        },
        Subscription: {
                bookAdded: {
                        subscribe: () => pubsub.asyncIterator('bookAddedTopic')
                }
        }
};
module.exports = resolvers;
```

## 5.6.3 Server

Some more extensive changes are necessary in the server implementation. To realize subscriptions, we need bidirectional

68

communication, which is realized by WebSockets [1]. We need to bind the GraphQL Subscription endpoint to the WebSocket protocol instead of HTTP. Thus the HTTP listener

```
server.listen(PORT, () => console.log(`GraphQL on port ${PORT}`));
```

is removed and replaced by a websocket listener:

```
const ws = createServer(server);
ws.listen(PORT, () => {
    console.log(`GraphQL Server is now running on http://localhost:${PORT}`);
    new SubscriptionServer({
        execute,
        subscribe,
        schema
    },{
    server: ws,
        path: '/subscriptions'
    }
    );
});
```

In addition, a couple of new libraries need to be imported. This all adds up to the following source code in **server.js**:

```
var express = require('express');
var {graphqlExpress,graphiqlExpress} = require('graphql-server-express');
var bodyParser = require('body-parser');
var schema = require('./schema.js');
var {execute, subscribe} = require('graphql');
var {createServer} = require('http');
var {SubscriptionServer} = require('subscriptions-transport-ws');

const PORT = 4000;
const server = express();
server.get('/', function (req, res) {  res.send('Hello World!');});
server.use('/graphql', bodyParser.json(), graphqlExpress({ schema }));
server.use('/graphiql', graphiqlExpress({
   endpointURL: '/graphql',
   subscriptionsEndpoint: `ws://localhost:${PORT}/subscriptions`
}));

const ws = createServer(server);
ws.listen(PORT, () => {
   console.log(`GraphQL Server is now running on http://localhost:${PORT}`);
   new SubscriptionServer({
      execute,
      subscribe,
      schema
   },{
      server: ws,
      path: '/subscriptions'
   }
   );
});
```

## 5.6.4 Testing

To test whether our server is working, let's open the address `http://localhost:4000/graphiql` in two browser windows (representing client 1 and client 2).

### 5.6.4.1 Subscription Request

Client 1 subscribes to the `bookAdded` event. It expects to receive both `id` and `title` of the newly added book, once an event is triggered. Let's execute the following subscription request in client 1.

```
subscription{
  bookAdded{
    id
    title
  }
}
```

### 5.6.4.2 Subscription Response

The immediate response sent to client 1 should be

```
"Your subscription data will appear here after server publication!"
```

This response, however, is not static, a new response will be provided as soon as the graph data is modified and a book is added.

### 5.6.4.3 Mutation Request

In a second browser window, we simulate client 2. It will trigger the event, by sending the following `addBook` mutation.

```
mutation {
  addBook(title: "The New Book"){
    id
    title
  }
}
```

### 5.6.4.4 Mutation Response

Client 2 should immediately receive the following response with the newly created book, including its title and the unique id.

```
{
  "data": {
    "addBook": {
      "id": "5",
      "title": "The New Book"
    }
  }
}
```

### 5.6.4.5 Subscription Response

At the same time, client 1 in the first browser window should also receive a notification for the added book data, including its title and the unique id.

```
{
  "bookAdded": {
    "id": "5",
    "title": "The New Book"
  }
}
```

# 6 GraphQL Best Practices

A number of best practices have been established that provide some guidance to the implementers of GraphQL APIs. We list a number of best practices from the areas of binding to network protocols and data formats, versioning, authorization, caching and handling long lists including pagination.

## 6.1 Protocol Binding and Data Format

GraphQL is used for building distributed systems, so we need to talk about how data is sent from a client to a server and back. Which protocols are involved and how is the data serialized?

Typically, we would use a GraphQL runtime, which handles the protocol binding, serialization, and deserialization. The requests and responses are bound to the HTTP protocol and the JSON data format is used for serialization. We study how to bind requests in section 6.1.1 and how to bind responses in section 6.1.2.

### 6.1.1 HTTP Request Binding

On the server-side, there is a single generic HTTP endpoint (`/graphql`) that receives the various GraphQL requests that clients send to the server. A GraphQL request that is sent to the GraphQL endpoint consists of the following components:

- the query/mutation/subscription, written in the GraphQL query language (see chapter 3).

- the list of variables

- the name of the operation

A GraphQL request can be mapped to an HTTP request with JSON data structures in two ways: (1) In the form of an HTTP GET with query parameters, as shown in section 6.1.1.1, or (2) in the form of an HTTP POST with a JSON document, as shown in section 6.1.1.2.

## 6.1.1.1 HTTP GET Request Binding

If the request is bound to an HTTP GET method, query parameters are used to encode the GraphQL query, variables, and operation name. The query is simply an expression in the GraphQL query language. The operation name is a simple string. The variables are a JSON object, which contains key-value pairs for variable-name and variable-value. This object is serialized according to JSON serialization rules. The result looks as follows.

```
HTTP GET /graphql
?query={customers{name}}
&operationName=op
&variables"={"var1":"val1","var2":"val2}
```

## 6.1.1.2 HTTP POST Request Binding

If the request is bound to an HTTP POST, a JSON document is used to encode the GraphQL query, variables, and operation name. Note that everything is serialized according to JSON rules, except for the value of the query field. It is a string, and this string is serialized according to the rules of the GraphQL query language. The result looks as follows.

```
HTTP POST /graphql
Content-Type: application/json
{""
  query: "{customers{name"}},""
  operationName: ""op,""
  variables: {""
    var1":"val1,""
```

```
   var2":"val2
 }
}
```

## 6.1.2 HTTP Response Binding

GraphQL responses are mapped to HTTP responses with a
JSON payload, whether the response returns an error or actual data. When actual data is returned, the payload is a JSON
object with the name **data** on the top-level. This object contains
the objects and attributes that were requested in the query/mu-
tation/subscription.

```
HTTP 200 OK
Content-Type: application/json
{
  "data": {""
    customers:[
      {""
        name":"Joe
      },
      {""
        name":"Bill
      }
    ]
  }
}
```

When processing the GraphQL request fails, a list of errors is
returned. Each error is detailed with further information, such
as a message containing more detail.

```
HTTP 200 OK
Content-Type: application/json
{"
  errors": [
    {""
      message: "An error "occurred
    }
  ]
}
```

# 6.2 Versioning

Successful software always
gets changed.

*Frederick P. Brooks*

Managing change and evolution in software systems is never
easy, but it is especially difficult to manage change in loosely-
coupled distributed systems, such as API solutions. Already a
small change in the API is enough to break some of the clients
consuming the API. From the perspective of the API consumer,
longevity and stability are important aspects of published APIs.
When APIs are published, they become available for consumers
and it has to be assumed that the consumers build apps with the
APIs. Published APIs cannot be changed in an agile manner.
At least, APIs need to stay backward (and forward) compatible,
so that old clients do not break and new clients can use the new
and improved features.

## 6.2.1 Types of API Changes

People may want to change various aspects of published APIs.
Are all of these changes equally severe for the clients? In this
section, we analyze potential changes and classify them according to their severity. Severe changes are those changes that are
incompatible (see section 6.2.1.2) and break a client. Not so severe are those API changes, that do not impact the client. They
are called backward compatible (see section 6.2.1.1).

### 6.2.1.1 Backward Compatible Changes

An API is backward compatible if an unchanged client can interact with a changed API. The unchanged client should be able
to use all the functionality that was offered by the old API. If a

change is supposed to be backward compatible, certain changes to the API are prohibited, while others are possible. The following is a list of backward compatible changes:

- Adding fields

- Adding types

- Adding queries, mutations, and subscriptions

### 6.2.1.2 Incompatible Changes

If a change to the API breaks the client, the change was incompatible. In general, removing and changing aspects of the API leads to incompatibilities. Here is a non-exhaustive list of incompatible changes:

- Removing existing fields

- Changing existing fields

- Removing types

- Removing queries, mutations or subscriptions

## 6.2.2 No Versioning in GraphQL APIs

Since evolution is difficult to manage, APIs should ideally be built in such a manner, that evolution becomes practically unnecessary and that any foreseeable changes can be realized as compatible changes. The versioning issue in GraphQL is not as severe as in other philosophies for building APIs. In GraphQL, the client needs to decide on the shape of the response when sending a request. A GraphQL API only returns the fields that are explicitly requested by the client.

Of course, the client can only choose from the available fields. GraphQL supports building backward compatible APIs. This means, that additional fields, additional types, additional queries, mutations, and subscriptions can be added. But existing fields cannot be changed or removed. No fields can be removed from existing types, and no types queries, mutations or subscriptions can be removed.

An often-raised concern of avoiding versioning is that we have to deal with ever-growing API responses, as evolution allows for adding, but not for removing fields. With GraphQL the impact is much smaller: Only the size of the schema would grow and it might be harder to find the right field that is needed in the given situation. But the size of the actual response would not automatically grow when the schema grows since the response only contains the fields which are explicitly requested by the client.

## 6.3 Number of APIs

How many GraphQL APIs should a company have? The power of GraphQL can only be fully utilized if all relevant data is within the same graph. As much data as possible should be linked to the same graph. This graph can then be exposed in one GraphQL API. It thus makes sense to have the complete API portfolio in one and the same GraphQL API.

## 6.4 Authentication and Authorization

Two similar terms -- authentication and authorization -- are used in the context of API security. For the following discussion, it is essential to know the distinction between the two. *Authentication* is a concept for answering the question: Who are you? Authentication is a method for providing proof of the claimed identity. *Authorization* is a concept that answers the question: What are you allowed to do? Authorization provides the rights assigned to the confirmed identity, for example access rights. Authentication is a precondition for proper authorization.

GraphQL does not prescribe how authentication or authorization should be implemented. But best practices for implementing both authentication and authorization can be observed.

### 6.4.1 Authentication

It is best practice to handle authentication in the HTTP server, e.g. in express. Any standard framework for authentication, preferably a token-based mechanism, such as OAuth[7, 2], may be used by the HTTP server. The token or the user object may then be passed in the context object to the GraphQL resolver function (see section 4.1.2.2).

### 6.4.2 Authorization

A good place for enforcing authorization is the business logic layer (see section 4.2), i.e. the layer between the resolve function in the GraphQL layer and the database layer. To handle authorization, the business layer needs information on the authenticated user. It can receive this via a user object that is passed to the business layer from the server, through the resolver function and the context object (see section 6.4.1).

## 6.5 Caching

GraphQL could be inefficient with respect to its connection to the backend. This is due to the structure of the resolver. The structure of the resolver allows for writing clean code on the server, where every field on every type has a dedicated function for resolving the respective value. A naive implementation of this clean concept would result in a rather inefficient implementation with a database access for each field.

A solution could be batching of multiple backend requests and caching the responses for all fields of the object. Facebook has published its *dataloader library* for this purpose. It allows for building up a business layer that can handle caching.

Caching requires an identifier. In REST, HTTP caching is used and the query path is used for identifying objects. Sometimes type specific identifiers are used since they are easily available in database tables. In GraphQL the query path is not a unique identifier. The same object can be accessed using various query paths. Thus, it is preferred to use globally unique identifiers and not type specific ones for caching.

# 6.6 Long Lists and Pagination

There are a couple of conventions for handling long lists in GraphQL: Plurals, Slices, and Pagination. Let's have a closer look at these options.

## 6.6.1 Plurals

When modeling a 1:n relation in the schema, we use a field with a name in plural form. This is where Plurals got their name. Plurals are realized as arrays. Plurals actually do not employ any form of pagination.

In the following example, we use a plural to model the relation between the query type and the book type.

```
type Query {
  books: [Book]
}
type Book {
  id: ID!
  title: String
}
```

The following query uses the plural to retrieve all the books.

```
query {
  books {
    title
```

```
        id
    }
}
```

## 6.6.2 Slicing

Slicing is introduced to limit the data that is returned:   retrieving only the first two/three/four etc. books, or only the last two/three/four etc. is an example of a slice of the data.   This slicing approach can be used for pagination, as we can retrieve the first two, then the next two, then the next two in slices. Slicing can be realized with an offset (see section 6.6.3), or with a cursor (see section 6.6.4).

## 6.6.3 Slicing with Offset

It is best practice to use the parameters **first** and **after** for slicing in GraphQL. The parameter **first** specifies the size of the page, i.e. the number of items on that page. The parameter **after** specifies either the index at which to start or the id of the element at which to start. Receiving the two books after book number three corresponds to the following query.

```
query {
  books(first: 2, after: 3) {
    title
        id
  }
}
```

Slicing with offset, based on the parameters **first** and **after**, does not exist out of the box. It needs to be implemented in the resolver function (see sections 4.1.2.2 and 5.3.1) of **books()**.

## 6.6.4 Slicing with Cursor

When using pagination, we need to model the point in the list where the last page ends and the next page starts. This allows us to retrieve only the data that exists after the data we have

81

already retrieved. So far we have used an offset for this purpose. A cursor is a more flexible concept than an offset. Offsets may be skewed if a new element is added to the list or deleted from the list. Relying on an offset may cause us to read the same element multiple times or jumping over a bunch of elements. This is especially bad if the rate of change on the list is higher than the rate at which we read elements from the list. So instead of relying on the position in the list, cursors rely on the identity of an element, often an attribute with name id.

Where are cursors placed? We do not want to make them a part of the business object, since a business object may be a part of several cursored lists. This is why we introduce an indirection. The indirection is an explicit representation of the page, with a list of business objects to be shown on the page and meta data. The meta data includes the cursor for the next page, the cursor for the first page, and the cursor for the last page and whether a next page exists at all.

To create a cursor, the value of the id is typically base64 encoded. A query with a cursor on the book with id=''0001'' translates to MDAwMQ==.

```
query {
  books(first: 2, after: MDAwMQ==) {
    nodes {
      node {
        title
            id
      }
      cursor
    }
    pageInfo {
      startCursor
      nextCursor
      endCursor
      hasNextPage
    }
  }
}
```

This query might return the following:

```
{
  "data": {
    "books": {
      "nodes": [
        {
```

82

```
            "node": {
                "title": "API Architecture"
                "id": "0002"
            },
            "cursor": "MDAwMg=="
        },
        {
            "node": {
                "title": "RESTful API Design"
                "id": "0003"
            },
            "cursor": "MDAwMw=="
        }
    ],
    "pageInfo": {
        "startCursor": "MDAwMA==",
        "nextCursor": "MDAwNA==",
        "endCursor": "MDAxMA==",
        "hasNextPage": true
    }
}
}
}
}
}
```

The business objects on the page are modeled as objects called node. Each business object has an individual cursor. Additional meta data is modeled in a pageInfo object with the fields startCursor, nextCursor, endCursor and hasNextPage.

# Appendix

## Acknowledgements

The author would like to thank Prof. Dr. Dominik Gruntz for his valuable input to this book.

## Feedback

If you enjoyed this book and got some value from it, it would be great if you could share with others what you liked about the book on the Amazon review page. If you feel something was missing or you are not satisfied with your purchase, please contact me at matt@api-university.com. I read this email personally and am very interested in your feedback.

## About the Author

Matthias has provided expertise to international and national companies on software architecture, software development processes, and software integration. At some point, he got a PhD.

Nowadays, Matthias uses his background in software engineering to help com panies to realize their digital transformation agenda and to bring innovative software solutions to the market. He also loves sharing his knowledge in the classroom, at workshops, and in his books. Matthias is an instructor at the API-University, publishes a blog on APIs, is author of several books on APIs and regularly speaks at technology conferences.

# Other Products by the Author

## Book on Serverless GraphQL with Amazon's AWS Appsync

This book shows you how you can get up and running with serverless GraphQL in the cloud.

Since Facebook, Flickr and Shopify have built successful APIs with GraphQL, many companies consider following in the technological footsteps of these tech giants. GraphQL is great, but requires the manual installation of software infrastructure components, configuration, and some manual tweaking, especially if you want to scale the system up and down dynamically depending on the load.

AppSync is a cloud-based platform for developing GraphQL applications. It allows you to publish your first GraphQL API within minutes. AppSync is a fully managed serverless offering by AWS (Amazon Web Services). With its usage-based price model, AppSync can get you started without any upfront investment and allows organizations to save thousands of dollars on computing costs.

We get to know AppSync with in-depth walkthroughs, screenshots, and complete code samples, the reader is guided through the step-by-step process of creating new functions, responding to infrastructure events, developing API backends, executing code at specified intervals, and much more.

Title: Serverless GraphQL with Amazon's AWS AppSync
Author: Matthias Biehl
Release Date: 2018
Length: ca. 100 pages
ISBN-13: 978-1717110701
https://api-university.com/books/graphql-aws-appsync

## Book on REST & GraphQL

What is the right way to build a cool new API? For a long time, REST was thought to be the only appropriate tool for building modern APIs. But in recent years, another tool was added to the toolbox, when Facebook published GraphQL, the philosophy, and framework powering its popular API. More and more tech companies tried GraphQL and adopted it as one of their philosophies for API design. Some built GraphQL API next to their existing REST API, some replaced their REST API with GraphQL, and even others ignored the GraphQL trend to focus only on their REST API.

But, not only the tech companies are divided. Following the discussions around REST and GraphQL, there seem to be two camps of gurus leading very emotional discussions: "always use the hammer," one camp proclaims. "NO, always use the screwdriver," the other camp insists. And for the rest of us? Unfortunately, this situation is confusing, leading to paralysis and indecision about API design.

The intention of this book is to clear up the confusion and enable us to make our own decision. For our own API. By having the necessary criteria and background info, we can choose if the hammer or the screwdriver is better for our API project. This book will not say: use the hammer or use the screwdriver. Instead, this book will enable us to make a smart, reasonable and case-specific decision, a decision tailored to the specific API we are designing.

Title: REST & GraphQL - A Discussion on API Design
Author: Matthias Biehl
Release Date: 2018
Length: ca. 100 pages
ISBN-13: 978-1717109378
https://api-university.com/books/rest-graphql

## Book on RESTful API Design

Looking for Best Practices in RESTful APIs? This book is for you! Why? Because this book is packed with best practices on many technical aspects of RESTful API Design, such as the correct use of resources, URIs, representations, content types, data formats, parameters, HTTP status codes and HTTP methods.

You want to design and develop APIs like a Pro? Use API description languages to both design APIs and develop APIs efficiently. The book introduces the two most common API description languages RAML and OpenAPI/Swagger.

Your APIs connect to legacy systems? The book shows best practices for connecting APIs to existing backend systems.

You expect lots of traffic on your API? The book shows you how to achieve high security, performance, availability and smooth evolution and versioning.

Your company cares about its customers? Learn a customer-centric design and development approach for APIs, so you can design APIs as digital products.

Title: RESTful API Design
Author: Matthias Biehl
Release Date: 2016-08-30
Length: 290 pages
ISBN-13: 978-1514735169
https://api-university.com/books/api-design

## Book on Webhooks

Got RESTful APIs? Great. API consumers love them. But today, such RESTful APIs are not enough for the evolving expectations of API consumers. Their apps need to be responsive, event-based and react to changes in near real-time.

This results in a new set of requirements for the APIs, which power the apps. APIs now need to provide concepts such as events, notifications, triggers, and subscriptions. These concepts are not natively supported by the REST architectural style.

The good thing: we can engineer RESTful APIs that support events with a webhook infrastructure. The bad thing: it requires some heavy lifting. The webhook infrastructure needs to be developer-friendly, easy to use, reliable, secure and highly available.

With the best practices and design templates provided in this book, we want to help you extend your API portfolio with a modern webhook infrastructure. So you can offer both APIs and events that developers love to use.

Title: Webhooks - Events for RESTful APIs
Author: Matthias Biehl
Release Date: 2017-12-22
Length: 130 pages
ISBN-13: 978-1979717069

https://api-university.com/books/webhooks

## Book on API Architecture

Looking for the big picture of building APIs? This book is for you!

Building APIs that consumers love should certainly be the goal of any API initiative. However, it is easier said than done. It requires getting the architecture for your APIs right. This book equips you with both foundations and best practices for API architecture. This book presents best practices for putting an infrastructure in place that enables efficient development of APIs. This book is for you if you want to understand the big picture of API design and development, you want to define an API architecture, establish a platform for APIs or simply want to build APIs your consumers love. What is API architecture? Architecture spans the bigger picture of APIs and can be seen from several perspectives: The architecture of the complete solution, the technical architecture of the API platform, the architecture of the API portfolio, the design decisions for a particular API proxy. This book covers all of the above perspectives on API architecture. However, to become useful, the architecture needs to be put into practice. This is why this book covers an API methodology for design and development. An API methodology provides practical guidelines for putting API architecture into practice. It explains how to develop an API architecture into an API that consumers love.

Title: API Architecture
Author: Matthias Biehl
Release Date: 2015-05-22
Length: 190 pages
ISBN-13: 978-1508676645

https://api-university.com/books/api-architecture

## Book on OpenID Connect

What is the difference between OAuth 2 and OpenID Connect?

For API security there are two standards — and they both start with O. So it is no wonder, people ask all the time what the difference between the two is.

If you have read the OAuth 2 Book, you already know a lot about OAuth. The OAuth standard ensures that there is no unintended leakage of information about the resource owner to the client. For example, it is ensured that the client does not get hold of the resource owner's credentials. The OAuth standard ensures the privacy of the resource owner. However, there are cases, where the client should have the possibility to get access to specific profile information of the resource owner.

Title: OpenID Connect - Identity Layer for you API

Author: Matthias Biehl

Release Date: 2018-05-30

Length: 90 pages

ISBN-13: 978-1979718479

https://api-university.com/books/openid-connect

## Book on Oauth 2.0

This book offers an introduction to API Security with OAuth 2.0. In less than 80 pages you will gain an overview of the capabilities of OAuth. You will learn the core concepts of OAuth. You will get to know all 4 OAuth Flows that are used in cloud solutions and mobile apps. If you have tried to read the official OAuth specification, you may get the impression that OAuth is complicated. This book explains OAuth in simple terms. The different OAuth Flows are visualized graphically using sequence diagrams. The diagrams allow you to see the big picture of the various OAuth interactions. This high-level overview is complemented with a rich set of example requests and responses and an explanation of the technical details. In the book, the challenges and benefits of OAuth are presented, followed by an explanation of the technical concepts of OAuth. The technical concepts include the actors, endpoints, tokens and the four OAuth flows. Each flow is described in detail, including the use cases for each flow. Extensions of OAuth - so called profiles - are presented, such as OpenID Connect and the SAML2 Bearer Profile. Sequence diagrams are presented to explain the necessary interactions.

Title: Oauth 2.0 - Getting Started in Web-API Security
Author: Matthias Biehl
Release Date: 2014-11-15
Length: 76 pages
ISBN-13: 978-1507800911
https://api-university.com/books/oauth-2-0-book

## Online Course on OAuth 2.0

Securing APIs is complicated? This course offers an introduction to API Security with OAuth 2.0. In 3 hours you will gain an overview of the capabilities of OAuth. You will learn the core concepts of OAuth. You will get to know all 4 OAuth flows that are used in cloud solutions and mobile apps. You will also be able to look over the shoulder of an expert using OAuth for the APIs of Facebook, LinkedIn, Google and Paypal.

Title: OAuth 2.0 - Getting Started in Web-API Security

Lecturer: Matthias Biehl

Release Date: 2015-07-30

Material: Video, Workbooks, Quizzes

Length: 4h

https://api-university.com/courses/oauth-2-0-course

## Online Course on RESTful API Design

Looking for best practices of RESTful API Design? This course is for you! Why? This course provides interactive video tutorials on the best practices of RESTful design. These best practices are based on the lessons learned from building and designing APIs over many years.

The course also includes video lectures on technical aspects of RESTful API Design, including the correct use of resources, URIs, representations, content-types, data formats, parameters, HTTP status codes and HTTP methods. And thanks to many interactive quizzes, learning REST becomes an engaging and exciting game-like experience.

We focus on the practical application of the knowledge, to get you ready for your first RESTful API project. The course includes guided mini-projects to get you ready for the practical application of REST.

After completing this course, you will be able to design RESTful APIs – but not just any APIs, you have all the knowledge to design APIs, which your consumers will love.

Title: RESTful API Design

Lecturer: Matthias Biehl

Release Date: 2018-05-01

Material: Video, Workbooks, Quizzes

Length: 3h

https://api-university.com/courses/restful-api-design-course

# Bibliography

[1] The WebSocket API. Technical report, W3C, September 2012. 5.6.3

[2] Matthias Biehl. *OAuth 2.0: Getting Started in Web-API Security (API University Series) (Volume 1)*. CreateSpace Independent Publishing Platform, 1 edition, January 2015. 6.4.1

[3] Matthias Biehl. *RESTful API Design: Best Practices in API Design with REST (API-University Series Book 3)*. 1 edition, August 2016. 4.3.1.3

[4] Matthias Biehl. *Webhooks - Events for REST APIs*, volume 4 of *API-University Series*. December 2017. 3.5

[5] Matthias Biehl. *REST and GraphQL - A Discussion on API Design*, volume 7 of *API-University Series*. 2018. 1.6

[6] Lee Byron. GraphQL specification. Technical report, Facebook, October 2016. 1.2

[7] Dick Hardt. The OAuth 2.0 authorization framework. Technical Report 6749, RFC Editor, Fremont, CA, USA, October 2012. 6.4.1

# Index

## S

Scalar Types, 20
Scalar Types, built-in, 20
Scalar Types, custom, 20
Schema, 17
Schema Definition Language,
    14
Schema Language, 13, 17
Security, 47
SELECT, 28
Slicing, 81
SOAP, 12
Stability, 47
Subscription, 26, 35
Syntax-directed Editing, 18

## T

Type Graph, 17
Type Name, 18
Type System, 17
Types, 18

## U

Union, 22

## V

Variables, 33
Verification, 46

## W

Webhooks, 35
WebSocket, 40, 69
WHERE, 30

Made in the USA
San Bernardino, CA
03 June 2018